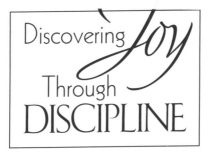

Discovering *Joy* Through DISCIPLINE

Elisabeth Elliot

GATEWAY
TO JOY

DISCOVERING JOY THROUGH DISCIPLINE
Back to the Bible Publishing
Copyright © 1992 by Elisabeth Elliot

International Standard Book Number
0-8474-0883-3

Edited by Rachel Derowitsch
Cover art by Robert Greuter & Associates

For information:
GATEWAY TO JOY
Post Office Box 82500
Lincoln, Nebraska 68501
2 3 4 5 6 7 8 9 10—04 03 02 01 00 99 98

Printed in the USA

CHAPTER ONE

"Abide in My Word"

The Price of Discipline

I don't know anybody who particularly likes the word *discipline*. Yet I believe that a disciplined life is a happy life, especially if our motivation is right—if it is for God's sake.

My second husband, Addison Leitch, spent many years on college campuses. And he observed that the happiest students were the musicians and the athletes, for they had voluntarily put themselves under authority.

When a student decides to join the marching band or the orchestra or to play football, he voluntarily puts himself under the authority of somebody who is going to tell him exactly what to do.

I believe that a disciplined life is a happy life, especially if our motivation is right— if it is for God's sake.

A football player is not doing "his own thing." He's under the authority of the coach, who is under the authority of the rule book. The size of the field, the shape of the goalposts, the kind of ball—that has all been determined by somebody else.

When the orchestra plays Bach, each musician is under the authority of the conductor. And the conductor is under the authority of Bach himself. There is a score to follow— it's somebody else's direction.

To find success and fulfillment, both the football player and the orchestra member must be committed to obedience. And so must we, if we are to find fulfillment in our quest to know God.

What does it mean to know God? It means walking with Him, talking with Him, living with and for Him. It means trusting and obeying Him.

There are several reasons why we obey God. First, He is God. Second, He made us. And third, obedience is the only route to fulfillment. There is no greater joy than the realization, *This is what I was made for.* We were made to glorify God. He has made us in His image. So as we do the things we were made to do, as we obey Him, we find the fulfillment the world is so desperately and so futilely searching for.

How often have we heard people say, "I'd give anything in the world if I could play football like so-and-so," or, "I'd give anything in the world if I could play the piano like that." Usually we mean that we would give anything but what it takes.

Would we give anything to know God, or is the price too high? Surrender is the price—learning the scales, practicing the game, toughening up. For us to surrender gladly to God's discipline, we need to be absolutely convinced that we are loved with an everlasting love and that, even while we are being disciplined, underneath are the everlasting arms.

God says, "As many as I love, I rebuke and chasten" (Rev. 3:19). Do you feel as if God has forsaken you today? Are you tempted to say, "God doesn't love me"? Do you cry with the psalmist, "Has God forgotten to be gracious? Has He in anger shut up His tender mercies?" (Ps. 77:9). No, He loves you. Don't imagine when you're being disciplined by God that He doesn't love you.

Discipline is surrender. And the only reason we surrender to another person is that we believe he knows something we don't know and that he can help us do something we want to do. Certainly God knows far more than we do about our fulfillment and how we can reach it. And He can lead us to fulfillment in a way we could never achieve by ourselves.

God calls us, but we are free to disobey Him. The tides and the winds are not free to disobey. The storms occur at the bidding of God. But He has given us the power to choose to love and obey Him or to reject and disobey Him. My fulfillment depends on my answer to His call. Will I do what He wants me to do, or will I do my own thing?

You've probably heard John 8:32 quoted as often as I have: "The truth shall make you free." But there is an essential condition that prefaces these words of Jesus. He said, "If you abide in My word, you are My disciples indeed. And you shall know the truth, and the truth shall make you free" (vv. 31–32).

Truth leads to freedom only when it is obeyed. Try telling the secular mind that liberation comes from obedience, from submission to authority, from discipline. To the world's mind that makes no sense. But the Bible says that freedom lies on the far side of obedience.

God calls us, but we are free to disobey Him. He has given us the power to choose to love and obey Him or to reject and disobey Him.

The words *disciple* and *discipline* both come from the Latin word meaning "to learn." We are learners. Disciples are those who answer God's call. And self-discipline is their way of saying to God, "Speak, Lord, Your servant is listening. I'll do what You say." Discipline is a wholehearted yes, a glad surrender to our loving Master, whose will is our peace.

Second Timothy 1:7 says, "God has not given us a spirit of fear, but of power and of love and of a sound mind." A sound mind is a disciplined mind. The Spirit of God inspires self-discipline. There is no dichotomy between self-discipline and the Spirit of God. It is He who inspires it.

Paul goes on to tell Timothy, "Therefore do not be ashamed of the testimony of our Lord, nor of me His prisoner, but share with me in the sufferings for the gospel according to the power of God" (v. 8).

Discipline is our response to God, our wholehearted yes to His will.

CHAPTER TWO

"Present Your Bodies"

The Discipline of the Body

Jesus made it clear that there are three conditions of discipleship. We must give up all right to ourselves, accept the cross and follow. In other words, surrender, accept and obey.

In giving up my right to myself, I have to realize that this body in which my "self" dwells is the only house I have on this earth in which to live. God gave me only one body. And I am responsible to take care of it in an honorable and responsible way for His glory. I don't belong to myself; I belong to Him. And I discipline my body for His sake.

The discipline of the body is sometimes called "mortification." That word comes from the same root as "mortal" or "mortician" and has to do with death and dying. Mortification is putting to death all that hinders my sanctification.

Physical and material things can be sanctified and made holy by being offered to God.

E. Herman, the author of a little book called *Creative Prayer*, says, "[Mortification] is not the sacrificing of the body to the alleged interests of the soul. It is the expression of the soul's regard for the body as an instrument of holiness."

What am I supposed to do to preserve my body as an instrument of holiness? I am to present it to God as an act of spiritual worship. Romans 12:1 says, "I beseech you therefore, brethren, by the mercies of God, that you present your bodies a living sacrifice, holy, acceptable to God, which is your reasonable service." Another translation says, "This is your spiritual act of worship" (NIV). How wonderful it is to think that this physical body, in its presentation to God, becomes a spiritual act of worship.

Christianity does not make a distinction between the physical and the spiritual, as though the physical is bad and the spiritual is good. Many religions do that, and often Christianity is accused of doing that. But that could not be further from the truth. We are very physical, very earthy. And we recognize that physical and material things can be sanctified and made holy by being offered to God.

I am responsible to care for my body. How do I do that? For one thing, I exercise sexual control. In 1 Thessalonians 4:3 we read, "You should abstain from sexual immorality." That covers every kind of sexual sin. The passage goes on to say, "That each of you should know how to possess his own vessel in sanctification and honor, not in passion of lust, like the Gentiles who do not know God" (vv. 4–5).

Have you ever thought about the near obsession Americans have with eating and drinking? The minute we get on an airplane, everybody is wondering, *When are they going to come down the aisle with the drinks? Will there be peanuts? Will there be a snack? Will there be a meal?*

Everywhere we go we find vending machines. Offices now have kitchens equipped with microwaves and coffeemakers. Some of that may be very wise; it would save a lot of time and money if these were used only for lunch. But I suspect that much of their use is just for unnecessary snacking.

I'm not trying to reform the appetite of the whole world. But I do want to help Christians gain control over their bodies, which are meant to be hallowed and sanctified for God. Maybe you need to think about whether you're getting too much sugar, soft drinks, candy, snack foods, salt or fats.

If you have been weak here, think what you need to do to begin the discipline of eating and drinking. I don't know, and maybe you don't either. But God can help you with it. Have you prayed about it? Have you seriously asked God to enable you to cut down where you need to cut down? Perhaps a good place to start would be by fasting for a day or two. Maybe you just need to give up between-meal snacks. Or maybe you need to go on a full-fledged diet. Pray for God's guidance.

If you're going to do the work God has given you to do, you also need to get the right amount of sleep. Getting up in the morning takes discipline, but so does going to bed at night. And most people's trouble with getting up in the morning is that they haven't gone to bed at a sensible hour.

But that may mean giving up a lot of things you might enjoy doing in the evening. Is this a spiritual issue? If sleep and diet keep you from doing what God wants you to do, they are spiritual issues.

And what are you like when you do get up in the morning? Do you rise joyfully, or are you a grouch who can't be spoken to until you've had your coffee? There's really no excuse for a Christian behaving in that way.

Are your first words to your family in the morning words of good cheer, or do they call attention to yourself and your misery and grumpiness about getting up? A great servant of God prayed, "Lord, make us masters of ourselves, that we may be the servants of others."

May the Lord enable us to hallow our bodies, to bring them under His mastery.

CHAPTER THREE

"Think Soberly"

The Discipline of the Mind

Not only are we to have disciplined bodies, but we're also to have disciplined minds. One writer said it takes discipline to "eliminate the disorder of the unnecessary." I want mine to be an orderly and clean mind that naturally turns away from the disorder of the unnecessary.

In 1 Peter 1:13 we read, "Therefore gird up the loins of your mind, be sober." Peter was writing to exiles, to people who had been scattered and who had suffered hot fires of trial to prove the quality of their faith. He told them to get rid of unnecessary clutter and distraction. He wanted them to develop holy minds.

Sir Joshua Reynolds gave three rules for developing a holy mind. First, meditate on God; hold your mind on Him. Second, think your way to a sober estimate of yourself (Rom. 12:3). And third, read books.

I want mine to be an orderly and clean mind that naturally turns away from the disorder of the unnecessary.

It's useless for us to try to empty our minds and think about nothing. There are exercises in meditation that are aimed at doing just that. But the Bible says we are to set our minds on Christ and listen to Him. That's entirely different from trying to empty our minds.

But Jesus did tell us what *not* to think about. He said, "Therefore do not worry about tomorrow, for tomorrow will worry about its own things. Sufficient for the day is its own trouble" (Matt. 6:34).

The past is gone; the future is not here. Both of those are God's business, not ours. If my mind is filled continuously with thoughts of the past, there's no room to concentrate on the job at hand. And if my mind is constantly worrying about the future—longing for something that hasn't come yet or may never come—then my energies will be dissipated. We need all the strength we can get to do the job God wants us to do now.

Do you think much about heaven and holiness and saints? Those things are much closer to what God created us to be than our present world is. So, the more we think about them, the more our minds will be transformed. As I get older, only a few things here on earth are important to me.

To meet our calling to be holy (see 1 Pet. 1:16), we need to be "renewed in the spirit of [our] mind" (Eph. 4:23). That takes setting our minds on Christ, having His mind. If we have the mind of Christ, how are we going to get along with the rest of the world? Not very well some of the time. The truth teller, as Socrates predicted even before Christ, will have his eyes gouged out.

In our "civilized" society, we don't gouge out eyes. We merely tell the man who turns from the broad road to the narrow that he's "holier-than-thou," a remark usually made with a degree of scorn. Or we use any other label that will exonerate the rest of us from the responsibility of being Christlike. We pity his naïveté, his narrowness, his unreality, never suspecting that there could be in our midst someone whose mind is set on things above because his "life is hidden with Christ in God" (Col. 3:3).

We need to change our conceptions of reality and of possibility. We need to see what Christ wants to do in others. Are your prayers for somebody else sometimes despairing?

Do you feel as if there isn't any chance in the world that he will ever change? Believe that he is redeemable. Ask God to give you the mind of Christ with regard to that person.

Knowing God's will requires total self-abandonment.

We also need to offer up our imaginations, to learn to think God's thoughts with Him. Are you perplexed today about discovering the will of God? There are three simple steps in Romans 12:1–2. First, "present your [body] a living sacrifice" (v. 1). Tell the Lord, "I'm all Yours; I'll do anything You say." Second, "do not be conformed to this world" (v. 2). Instead of running to the world for advice, run to God. Pray. Open your Bible. Seek His will. Third, "be transformed"—let God change you. *Then* you'll discover what He wants you to do.

Knowing God's will requires total self-abandonment— the presenting of your body—and the refusal to let the world squeeze you into its own patterns of thinking. Your behavior will change when your mind changes.

If we're going to change our concepts of reality and possibility, we must learn to distinguish between disagreement and hatred of the truth. There are times when people say to me, "You know, I disagree with a lot of the stuff you say." And I always ask, "Well, can you be specific? I need to know what you disagree with; I might be wrong." If what they disagree with is my simple quoting of a Scripture verse, then I think they're the ones in trouble.

If the Bible says, "Love your enemies," that means love your enemies (Matt. 5:44). It doesn't make any difference how powerful an enemy he may be or what awful thing he may have done to you. God commands us to love our enemies.

When writing to the young preacher Timothy, Paul said, "Teach and exhort these things. If anyone teaches otherwise

12

and does not consent to wholesome words, even the words of our Lord Jesus Christ, and to the doctrine which is according to godliness, he is proud, knowing nothing, but is obsessed with disputes and arguments over words, from which come envy, strife, reviling, evil suspicions, useless wranglings of men of corrupt minds and destitute of the truth" (1 Tim. 6:2-5).

May God give us the mind of Christ.

CHAPTER FOUR

"Honor All People"

The Discipline of Place

A friend called me some time ago to discuss a concern with me. She and her husband were growing dissatisfied with the sermons they were receiving at church, and she didn't quite know what to say to her pastor anymore. She wanted to be honest and also to *honor* him.

And I thought to myself, *Who thinks of honor nowadays?* We're told that we're all supposed to be equal. We introduce ourselves by first names only. We no longer use titles for people who once would have been considered our superiors. I have to confess as an old lady that it gives me a bit of a start when high school and college students call me Elisabeth. But that's the way it is nowadays. The idea of honor seems to have fallen on hard times.

But the Bible tells us to "honor all people" (1 Pet. 2:17). Another translation says to "give due honour to everyone" (New English Bible). If it's due, it's not above and beyond the call of duty; it's something we owe. Honor has nothing to do with our feelings about ourselves or about others.

The woman who called me may have thought that only a complimentary remark would honor her pastor. But sometimes telling the painful truth—in certain situations and after due consideration and prayer—may be the most honoring thing we can do. Surely we're not to flatter people or pay them compliments that are not honest. But it's difficult to respect and hold in high regard people who don't seem to deserve honor.

14

Part of our problem is that we're confused about the definition of respect. Respect means, first of all, reverence under God. It means a proper appreciation for the person God has made, for the simple reason that God made him. The Bible says that "God shows no partiality" (Acts 10:34). And James warns about judging people by false standards. He writes, "If you show partiality, you commit sin, and are convicted by the law as transgressors" (2:9).

Sometimes telling the painful truth—in certain situations and after due consideration and prayer— may be the most honoring thing we can do.

We're not to show partiality, but we do need to learn to discriminate. And that's another word that has fallen on hard times. Yet the Bible is very discriminating—it makes distinctions. We need to learn to do the same; making distinctions is entirely right and proper.

One key word that will help us understand some important distinctions is *due*. When Peter tells us to give due honor to everyone, he specifies three different ways of obeying that command: "*Love* the brotherhood. *Fear* God. *Honor* the king" (1 Pet. 2:17, emphasis mine). Honor is something that is given, never something we should take or demand for ourselves.

Another helpful word is *duty*. A duty is something that must be paid; it is an obligation. A wife has a duty to her family, to her husband and to her children. And duties differ. A husband's duty in the office differs from his duty to the church. His duty in the church differs from his civic duty and from his duty to the home. The fulfillment of those obligations is honor.

A couple about to be married asked me if there was one word I would want to give them that would help them build a happy marriage. And I gave them the word *honor*. When I forget that my husband is God's gift to me and that, even though he is a sinner who fails from time to time, I'm to honor him because he holds the office of a husband, then we're in trouble. And I must confess that I don't always treat my husband honorably.

Some women ask, "How can I honor my husband when he doesn't deserve it? If he's an alcoholic or if he's an abusive husband, does he deserve respect?" No, he doesn't deserve it, but he is to be honored because he is the husband.

But we also need to realize that not everybody has a right to everything. To honor a child is not to allow him to get away with murder; it is to discipline him, perhaps even to spank him. A child has a right to be taken care of and to be taught. But he does not have a right to vote, marry, be taxed—or to run the household!

We must not confuse superiority of position with superiority of worth. A father and mother are not worth more in God's sight than their little child. But they have been *given* a position above that of the child. They are in charge; they are responsible; they are obligated to discharge their duties for God's sake.

By the same token, an employer honors his employees by being fair and just, by paying them fair wages, by treating them kindly, by remembering that he has God as his master. Another example is Mother Teresa, who recognized the worth of those dying on the streets of Calcutta when others thought of them as refuse. She honored them.

Jesus said in Luke 6, "Just as you want men to do to you, you also do to them likewise. But if you love those who love you, what credit is that to you? For even sinners love those who love them. . . . But love your enemies, do good, and lend, hoping for nothing in return; and your reward will be great, and you will be sons of the Highest" (vv. 31–32, 35).

Let's ask the Lord to help us give honor where honor is due.

CHAPTER FIVE

"Wait on the Lord"

The Discipline of Time

Time is a created thing, a gift. We can't make any more of it. We can only receive it and be faithful stewards in our use of it. We can never say, "I couldn't do the will of God because I didn't have time."

Do you believe there is always time to do the will of God? If not, consider Psalm 31:15: "My times are in Your hand." When your plans seem to slip out of your hands, remember that your time never slips out of God's hands. Nothing slips out of His hands.

When your plans seem to slip out of your hands, remember that your time never slips out of God's hands. Nothing slips out of His hands.

Psalm 27:14 says, "Wait on the LORD; be of good courage, and He shall strengthen your heart; wait, I say, on the LORD!" I have three dates marked next to that verse in my Bible—1982, 1983 and 1984. I think at least two of those dates had to do with my mother, who was getting more and more feeble and senile. I was praying that the Lord would take her home quickly. In His providence, He did not take her home until 1987. So for those four or five years, the Lord was saying to me, "Wait for Me; be strong and take courage. My timing is never late. I know exactly what is best for your mother. Remember that I love your mother a whole lot more than you do."

There's always enough time to do God's will, and His timing is always perfect. Consider again the life of Jesus. Think of the pressure He faced—things to do, crowds of people following Him, people pressing Him with questions and arguments, people who believed Him and people who mocked Him, people who argued with Him and people who sought to kill Him.

Jesus went off by Himself into the hills to pray—and the multitudes followed Him. They reproached Him again and again for His absence. He was not always available when He was needed. And there's a lesson there for us. I talk so much about the need for us to be available to serve other people, to sacrifice and lay down our lives, to be broken bread and poured-out wine. But there are times when we have to be unavailable. And people will not always understand that.

Jesus must have left many "if onlys" behind. Remember the words of Mary and Martha: "If You had been here, my brother would not have died" (John 11:21, 32).

There are times when we have to be unavailable. And people will not always understand that.

Only the people who could get to Jesus were healed. Remember the four determined men who brought their friend on his bed? They were so determined to put him in Jesus' presence and get him healed that they actually went up on the roof and let their friend down through the tiles. But many others couldn't do that; they couldn't touch even the hem of His garment.

We have to leave things in God's hands. Jesus always did those things that pleased the Father, and He fulfilled all the work His Father had given Him to do (John 8:29; 17:4). We can't always do all the things other people would like us to do, and we're not required to. Jesus didn't do everything everybody expected Him to do either. The one rule of His life was to do the will of the Father. He was a man with a man's limitations—limitations of time and of space. But He did all that the Father wanted Him to do.

Maybe we need to pray, "Lord, enable me to finish the work *You* give me to do; and please give me discernment to know what is *Your* work and what is not." Concerning all the demands that come to my desk, I have to say constantly, "Lord, I don't know whether to say yes or no to this. Give me wisdom; give me discernment." We have the same limitations Jesus had. I don't believe that God wants us to be frantic or frustrated or harried or harassed or hassled.

Our problem is not that we have too little time but that we spend so poorly the time we are given.

Jesus said, "Come to Me, all you who labor and are heavy laden, and I will give you rest. Take My yoke upon you and learn from Me, for I am gentle and lowly in heart, and you will find rest for your souls. For My yoke is easy and My burden is light" (Matt. 11:28-30). Perhaps we're not gentle and humble in heart enough to come to Him in simplicity and humility, to lay down our burdens and say, "Lord, help me take Your burden, the light one. Help me take Your yoke, which is easy."

One thing that is not on God's list for me to do is worry. Worry is fruitless and disobedient; it's taking the not-given and refusing the given. God has given us only this minute. We often neglect the thing assigned because we are worried about the thing that is not yet our business. That's the opposite of trust, a wicked squandering of time and energy. Our problem is not that we have too little time but that we spend so poorly the time we are given.

Do you have time with God? Or do you say, "I can't possibly have much of a quiet time"? If you don't have time for a quiet time, you really are too busy. You need to have regular time with God—a special time for worship and thanksgiving and confession and petition and intercession. Maybe you need time to keep a journal. You certainly need time to read your Bible.

Are your times in His hands? Put them there; trust Him.

CHAPTER SIX

"Beware of Covetousness"

The Discipline of the Body

The Bible says, "Every good gift and every perfect gift is from above, and comes down from the Father of lights, with whom there is no variation or shadow of turning" (James 1:17). If God gives us things, then we should thank Him for them. But we need to ask ourselves whether we are living for visible things or for invisible things.

I have nothing but what I've received. I take only what's given and do what I'm responsible to do with it. The things that are given to us should be received with thanksgiving and should be made material for sacrifice. By that I mean we should offer everything back to God.

The things that are given to us should be received with thanksgiving and should be made material for sacrifice.

When you get up in the morning, do you thank God for sleep? For the ability to put your feet on the floor and stand? For hot water in the bathroom and cold water to drink? For the morning star? For the ability to work? For a place to work—for a job? All these things are gifts. And if I thank Him, then I'm offering them back to Him in thankfulness. "Lord, this body that You've made capable of sleeping

21

and capable of waking up and getting up in the morning; these hands to do the work You've given me to do; these eyes to see the work; this heart to be grateful to You—I give them all back to You." That is the life of thanksgiving.

Think about material possessions. It is said that Hudson Taylor, founder of the China Inland Mission, sorted through all his possessions once a year. Whatever he had not used in that year, he gave away. He believed he would be held accountable for what he kept, and if he had not needed something in a year's time, he saw no reason to keep it if someone else could use it.

I have tried to make it a rule of my own life that when a new piece of clothing comes into the house, an old one goes out. I don't want to jam the closets full and have clothes hanging there for years that never get taken off the hanger. If I can do without something for a year, I can probably do without it for the rest of my life. Somebody else should have it.

Some people would say, "Oh, but I might need it sometime." They are just hoarders, and others are throw-awayers. And, of course, they seem to marry each other. I've talked to many couples made up of one who is a pack rat or hoarder and the other who throws things away. That's the way it is in our family.

Think about all those mayonnaise jars you've been saving. If you do canning in the fall—if you preserve applesauce and tomatoes and other produce—then by all means save them, as long as you can fill them up. But if you've got 1,000 jars and you're going to use only 500 of them, maybe you need to get rid of some.

I know a woman who has cupboards full of cracked and chipped dishes, foil pans from frozen foods, plastic containers from cottage cheese and ice cream and disposable forks and spoons, enough to last until the Millennium.

Why do we cling to the unnecessary? Most of us have some area of our lives that is cluttered. Are you in bondage to clutter?

A young woman in Canada sat down next to me when I was sitting by the book table at a meeting. She said, "I need help."

I said, "With what?"

She said, "I live in a cluttered house. I've been married for only a year and, I mean, like, it's a mess. I mean, it's getting me down. What shall I do?"

What am I to say to somebody in two minutes when other people are waiting to talk to me? So I said, "Well, how about starting by cleaning out one drawer?"

May God give us wisdom to hold things lightly, to let things go, to give our attention to things that last forever.

She said, "Wait a minute. I don't think you understand me. We're not talking about drawers. We're talking about the floor of the living room. We can't walk across the living room."

That woman was in trouble.

Yes, God has given us all things richly to enjoy, but not to enjoy forever. We don't really enjoy them when we start hoarding them. Let's not treat visible, temporal things like eternal things. They're not to be lived for.

Do you have collections of things—china, thimbles or maybe those little globes with snow in them? I don't know what you may be collecting, and I'm certainly not saying you have to get rid of those things. But we do need to give some thought to what we're saving. Jesus said in Luke 12:15, "Take heed and beware of covetousness, for one's life does not consist in the abundance of the things he possesses."

May God give us wisdom to hold things lightly, to let things go, to give our attention to things that last forever, to *simplify* our lives for His glory.

CHAPTER SEVEN

"Do It Heartily"

The Discipline of Work

Do you hate work? Do you hate Mondays and live for Fridays? Something is wrong if a Christian hates work, and I would hope we could catch a new vision of the discipline of work and the blessing that work is. God worked six days and rested one—one day out of seven is exactly the way God arranged things for Himself and the way He has arranged things for us.

I think the Sabbath rest God prescribed for us should be a declaration of freedom. We are not workhorses. We are not bees that work seven days a week. We can declare the freedom to take a day off, to rest, to worship God—a day in which we do things differently from the other six days of the week.

The work God has given us to do should be received as a gift.

Some of you may not enjoy your work because it doesn't look very Christian to you. But what is Christian work? Simply, Christian work is work done by a Christian. I'm a Christian writer—not just because I write about "Christian" subjects. I don't always write about Christian subjects. But I am a writer who is a Christian. A Christian plumber is not a plumber who works with Christian drains or Christian wrenches. A Christian plumber is a Christian who does plumbing the way a Christian should do it.

The work God has given us to do should be received as a gift. We should thank Him for it and offer it back to Him. It's the offering back to God that hallows the work. If we understand this, we can see that nobody is excluded from serving God, and no task is beneath a Christian.

Most people throughout history did not have much choice in the work they did. A peasant had work he could not possibly avoid. The Indians in the jungle in Ecuador didn't have any options about what they should do. Survival was their goal. There was no virtue in their work; it was simply a necessity. But even the mundane duties we have should be done for God.

You remember that Jesus spoke about those who had fed Him when He was hungry, clothed Him when He was naked and visited Him when He was in prison and sick. He said that those who hear those words will ask, "When did we see You a stranger and take You in, or naked and clothe You? Or when did we see You sick, or in prison, and come to You?" And He will say, "Inasmuch as you did it to one of the least of these, My brethren, you did it to Me" (see Matt. 25:35-40). So it is always possible to do our work for God.

We should be willing to be used and to be used up, according to the will of God. It takes a lot of prayer to sort out the demands of neighbors and family and work. And I can't tell you what the balance is. But God can. How important it is to spend quiet time with Him, to listen to what He is trying to say to us. He might be trying to tell us it's time to give up certain things that we think of as duties.

Maybe you are thinking, *Oh, I wish I could do a great work for God. I wish I could be a great preacher or teacher or singer or writer. I wish I could do something really significant for God— evangelism, missionary work, service of some sort that would be recognized.* Where does a great work for God begin?

You probably remember Stephen from the Book of Acts because he was the first martyr. But how did he get to be a great preacher so filled with the Holy Spirit that he offended the secular mind and was stoned to death? He served tables and oversaw the distribution of money and food to a group of Greek and Jewish widows in the early church. Not too many men would want to take on such a job. It was Stephen's willingness to do the humble and distasteful thing that made it possible for him to become the great martyr.

Stephen had set his heart not on miracle working or being a brilliant apologist but on serving his Master. He would not have been willing to serve tables had he been ambitious to do a "great" work for God.

It was Stephen's willingness to do the humble and distasteful thing that made it possible for him to become the great martyr.

I don't always want to do what I've been called to do. And probably you don't either. When we become discouraged with our work, we need to pray, "Let the beauty of the LORD our God be upon us, and establish the work of our hands for us" (Ps. 90:17). There will be days when we do our work halfheartedly and other days when we do it despondently. But if it is soaked in prayer, we can disregard how we feel about it. The beauty of the Lord our God will be upon us, and He will establish the work of our hands.

I discovered the therapeutic value of work when my first husband, Jim Elliot, died. I was on a jungle mission station with no other missionaries. Every day was packed with duties. I had a ten-month-old baby. I had a house to keep and language work to do. There were Indians I needed to serve in various ways—teaching, doing medical work, helping in the church and school. I had an airstrip to keep cleared. Work was a blessing, and I found rest and refreshment in actually doing the will of God. He doesn't remove the heat and the burden from us, but He will give us the rest we need as long as we are His obedient workers.

When my second husband was dying, I found that cooking, planning menus, cleaning, taking care of his laundry and taking his trays and his medicine to him still had to be done no matter how I was feeling. And I thanked God for that privilege and found great healing and consolation in each simple, ordinary task.

Paul wrote in Colossians, "Whatever you do, do it heartily, as to the Lord and not to men, knowing that from the Lord you will receive the reward of the inheritance; for you serve the Lord Christ" (3:23–24).

Thank God for the work He has given you, and ask Him to help you to do it for His glory. Think of it—*you serve the Lord Christ*!

CHAPTER EIGHT

"Believe in Me"

The Discipline of Feelings

Often in question-and-answer periods following my talks in public, people will ask, "Do you feel comfortable with this or that?" That question always nettles me a bit. Where did we get this idea that everything has to be comfortable? God never promised us a bed of roses. He promised us a cross. He asked us to follow Him, and His way is often rugged and lonely.

We need to bring our feelings, like our thoughts, into captivity. Paul says we are to pull down strongholds and bring every thought into captivity to Christ (2 Cor. 10:4–5). My thoughts and my emotions often get mixed together. Years ago Ronald Knox wrote, "We have replaced 'I believe' with 'one does feel.'" And I think there's even a stronger tendency nowadays to live by our feelings than there was when Knox wrote that.

We need to bring our feelings, like our thoughts, into captivity.

Do you make your decisions on the basis of your feelings, your comfort, your temperament, your preferences? Or do you seek to make decisions on the basis of the mind God has given you and the heart that has determined in advance to do His will?

Daniel's God-directed will triumphed over his emotions. He had resolved when he went into the king's court not to defile himself with the king's food (Dan. 1:8). A "resolve" is not a mood. If I have resolved to do something, then circumstances should have nothing to do with my carrying it through.

When King Darius issued an edict that no one was to worship any god but the king himself, Daniel had to choose his will over his emotions (6:1-10). If he had chosen to follow his emotions, no doubt the story would have been about Daniel *without* the lion's den. But he was governed by will, governed by his choice to obey the will of God. His decision was carried out without regard to his emotions.

Somebody once said to me, "I don't see how in the world you can get rid of your emotions." I don't try to *get rid* of them. Disciplining a horse is not getting rid of the horse. It's bringing the horse under control of the reins. Nor is disciplining a child getting rid of the child. It's teaching the child to do what he ought to do. We cannot get rid of our emotions, but we can surrender them to God. And we might just as well express our feelings aloud to God, because He already knows our thoughts before we think them.

The Psalms are filled with expressions of emotion. Take Psalm 6:3–4, for example: "My soul also is greatly troubled; but You, O LORD—how long? Return, O LORD, deliver me! Oh, save me for Your mercies' sake!" That sounds like a cry from a pit, doesn't it?

True holiness does not mean reaching an exalted state where feeling no longer exists. Jesus had deep and tender feelings. Remember His kindness to children, His treatment of babies, His weeping when Lazarus died, His anger at the money changers and the Pharisees, His anguish of soul in Gethsemane. Again and again we see in Jesus' life the triumph of His will over His emotions. He was resolved to do His Father's will.

When we live by our feelings, we get caught in the trap of being governed by our own desires. Jude warns against men who try to mold their lives according to their own desires (1:12-16, Phillips). Do we insist on doing that? If we do, that's a denial of Jesus as Lord. Paul says, "Therefore, brethren, we are debtors—not to the flesh, to live according to the flesh. For if you live according to the flesh you will die; but if by the Spirit you put to death the deeds of the body, you will live" (Rom. 8:12–13). If we "cut the nerve of our instinctive actions" by obeying the Spirit, then we will be on our way to real living. We do that by the help of the Holy Spirit. He's there for us. We can ask Him to help us discipline unruly emotions.

We need to reject the idea that if we're not feeling spiritual or pious or religious, then it would be hypocritical to pray or to sing or to go to church. I don't know very many people who, when they pray, often experience warm, spiritual feelings, a rising of their spiritual temperature. But the person who persists in obedience, despite his feelings, is truly faithful.

Self-discipline is a sign of spiritual and emotional maturity.

Jesus said to His disciples on the eve of His departure from them, a time when they would naturally be very distressed, "Let not your heart be troubled; you believe in God, believe also in Me" (John 14:1). If we say, "My heart is troubled," Jesus' words indicate that we can bring those troubled feelings under His control.

Paul says, "The fruit of the *Spirit* is . . . *self*-control" (Gal. 5:22–23, emphasis mine). We shouldn't think that once the Holy Spirit takes over we don't have to do anything more. Nor should we think that self-control is possible without the Holy Spirit's help. The grace of God, by His Holy Spirit, goes to work on our nature, and in that nature He has put the possibility of control. But we have to bring   it into harmony with the Spirit. Self-discipline, in other words, is a sign of spiritual and emotional maturity.

Jesus said to Peter, "Do you love Me?" (John 21:15). And Peter didn't say, "Lord, I feel good about You." He said, "Lord, You know all things; You know that I love You" (v. 17). And Jesus didn't ask for a kiss or a hug or an embrace. He asked for the one valid proof of love—obedience. He said, "Feed My sheep" (v. 17). Jesus wasn't asking, "How do you feel about Me?" He was asking for action.

We're given the choice day by day to choose good and refuse evil. Feelings will not, as a rule, help us very much, although our impulses are not always bad. But more often than not, we have to choose between principle and impulse. The apostle Paul struggled with this same issue. He wrote, "To will is present with me, but how to perform what is good I do not find. For the good that I will to do, I do not do; but the evil I will not to do, that I practice" (Rom. 7:18–19). And that is a disarmingly accurate description of most of us.

But Peter says, "Rest your hope fully upon the grace that is to be brought to you at the revelation of Jesus Christ; as obedient children, not conforming yourselves to the former lusts, as in your ignorance" (1 Pet. 1:13–14). We rest our hope on Him, and we obey. And then our emotions will flow from obedience.

May God help us bring our emotions under the control of the Holy Spirit. We will enjoy a new and unimagined peace, order and serenity in our lives, a holy harmony.

Other resources from Elisabeth Elliot

Discipline: The Glad Surrender

What do the words *discipline, commitment* and *obedience* really mean? Elisabeth Elliot uses personal stories and biblical illustrations to bring you the true meaning of these words and equip you to do God's will joyfully.

#11689 $7.99

The Liberty of Obedience

How does freedom come from obedience…even when obedience to God makes little, if any, sense in our view? Elisabeth Elliot found liberty in obeying God's call to return to the same tribe three years after they had killed her husband, Jim Elliot.

#1163X $4.99